Pomegranate

poems by

Debra Spencer

Hummingbird Press
Santa Cruz, California

Library of Congress Control Number: 2004110704
ISBN: 0-9716373-8-5

Cover art by Juliette Aristides, *Pomegranate*
Cover design by Mark Wiens and Jesse Autumn
Quark by Ken Weisner

Hummingbird Press
2299 Mattison Lane
Santa Cruz, CA 95062-1821
www.hummingbirdpresspoetry.com

Printed in Canada

I sang in my chains like the sea.
Dylan Thomas

for my father

Contents

Songs in Every Tongue

Everybody Wants to Be Blond

First Decade

Water is not always warm.
If you lean too far out of the high chair, the floor will hit you in the head.
The leaves of geraniums smell better than the flowers.
The safest place to be is in my father's arms.
Every word has its own color.
Singing is like flying.

If you tell Candace Fields a secret, she keeps it.
Sometimes there's nothing to eat but turkey soup.
When they fall into the bathtub, library books make a big splash.
It takes a lot longer to fill a coffee can with shelled walnuts than it does to eat them.
It's worth walking all the way around the block to avoid Timmy Weems.
A baseball card over the hole in your shoe keeps your sock clean.
Everybody else asks their mom first.

Not everybody wears the same kind of underwear.
No matter how stuck the bread is, you can't stick your knife in the toaster.
A baloney sandwich smells like lunch at breakfast and like garbage at lunch.
If you're only as big as Taro Inoke, they can sew the finger back on.
If you beg hard enough, you'll get the white Keds.
Michael Gilroy's lips feel good against my cheek.

Even Taymor Johnson gets sunburned.
If you're one of the Schmutzes, you have to spit out your pomegranate seeds.
Boys like Louis Trachtenberg make fun of you but give you their cupcake.
I can think anything I like, and no one will ever know.
I'm going to die.

Los Angeles

Grandpa moved slowly, said what he pleased, hovered in his
house like cigar smoke, like the sound of a baseball game from
the television in the morning room, line drives and Vin Scully
striking the rattan chairs while Grandma sat in the living room
among her brass Chinese bells, the lamp with Confucius beaming
from the black lacquer table on the carpet where we sprawled,
playing fish with cards she kept for us in the oak desk next to
the dining room, the long table draped with white linen where
we all sat down to eat, the sun in the western windows shining
through blue glass onto the china, onto faces above corned beef
and cabbage, above cherry pie, laughter rising into the chandelier
whose light, after dusk, spilled out through filmy curtains onto
bushes and the sloping lawn down to the poplar trees whose
branches began high above the sidewalk, where our father carried
us in our pajamas (the smell of cigar clinging) through the dark
to the car, and we sped away, our parents silhouetted in the front
seat against the streetlamps as we drove among stop-and-go
rubies and emeralds rushing into the curve of the marble-veined
concrete freeway, while in the back window the city lay stretched
like a woman reclining, her rolling hips, the curves of her valleys, her
firm hills, a woman wearing strings and strings of diamonds.

Being a Twin

Some scientists have suggested that all left-handed singletons
may be survivors of a vanished-twin pair.
Lawrence Wright, "Double Mystery"

As a child I gave a name to her
who had no face but mine.
Even our mother knew
nothing of her.

I laid out clothes for her
before my first day of school.
I made a sign for our bedroom door,
including her name in my favorite color.
When I was worried she always
listened while I whispered
far into the night.

The older I got,
the more resigned I became
to being without her. Gradually
we stopped talking,
and she dimmed
to a shadow in the mirror
late at night, and now I seem

to have gotten over her death,
which must have happened so long ago
that the sound of my heart
is all that's left of her.

The Cello

for Candace Fields

My first grade teacher Mrs. Nail had a pinched face with a long
jaw and she poked her head forward when she walked, as though
always angry. With her big hands she tore up my first attempt
at writing because I had made all the letters backward. Do it
again the *right* way, she said.

I was six. I loved boys. I wanted to be one. My best friend
Candace and I played we were boys. We wore jeans and pushed
our sweatshirt sleeves up above our elbows like boys did. We
talked rough and loud, we swaggered, we threw things. If we got
knocked around, if we fell down, we didn't whine, even if it hurt.
We rolled in leaves, climbed trees, jumped off things, kicked the
ball hard. We insulted each other and laughed about it.

Mrs. Nail told us she had once played cello in a symphony
orchestra. The whole class stared at her. Brad Dolliver asked
her, When were you a boy? No woman played the cello, not in
an orchestra. I thought Mrs. Nail had magical powers, that she
could change herself into a boy at will, like a fairy godmother
changing a mouse into a horse.

Christine Jorgenson was a boy and then went to Sweden to
become a girl. I asked my mother what she was named when she
was a boy. My mother thought George, but she wasn't sure. I
asked who named her Christine. I thought she'd have to go back
to her mother to get her new girl's name. But my mother said
she just named herself.

The last time we dared to be boys was sixth grade. Then we got
breasts. We started to bleed. I thought about learning to play
the cello, but it looked too big and awkward to lug around.

The San Fernando Valley

In summer the crows flew away at sunrise
from their nests in the eucalyptus.
I woke into heat stirred by wings,
heat so thick I could lean back on it
and be held up. All morning
I lay in the grass breathing dampness,
while above me the dry heat lay
on the green fields and the bare rock
of the Santa Susanas. When I stood barefoot
on the asphalt under the pepper trees
I felt the hum of the city through the soles of my feet,
felt the road roll away south
through dry yellow hills to the beach.
At midday I waded through heavy air
that moved aside slowly to let me pass.
To lift my arms and legs against it
took all my will. By afternoon the heat
buzzed in my blood like a drug.
In the evening when the eucalyptus brushed the hot sky
and languid crows flew home, buoyed on heat,
the dust in the road lay thick, the air still
as though no one moved, anywhere.
Beyond the eucalyptus the Santa Susanas
seemed as close as my bedroom, where I lay
against the cool underbelly of night.
When I closed my eyes I rose and hovered on the thermals
like a crow looking down through hot air
at the shell-colored hills and dead gold weeds,
at fields with weeds cut and plowed, sprinklers on bare dirt,
fields faintly green, with a light mist of green,
high cornfields near the house where I lay
in love with the heat that held me.

The Monkey Box

I was new at school and had red leather shoes. Sandy and Karen wore Oxfords, black on white, and Debbi wore navy blue Keds. The sidewalk was veined with tiny cracks, crisscrossed by ants searching for water. It was September, the hottest month, and we kept to the shade, scuffling through leaves.

Our cotton dresses were limp from sweat and heat. I pushed up my bangs to let the hot air cool my forehead. Sandy and Karen had yellow hair, but Debbi and I had brown. Our knees were skinned from rollerskating, from when the wheels caught in the sidewalk cracks. Our fingers smelled of crayon. The edge of my left hand was smeared with pencil lead.

We scuffled along, and then the others screamed and jumped onto the grass. I froze and looked down but saw only ants and veined concrete under my peculiar shoes.

Monkey box! Sandy said, keeping her feet off the sidewalk. *You're standing in it!* Karen said. *Get out!* said Debbi. *Quick!* They showed me the concrete imprint directly under my feet that said John H. Thompson, Canoga Park, 1956. Debbi said, *Now you're a monkey for a week.* My stomach sank. Everyone would know I was a monkey. They'd stick bananas in my face at lunch, make monkey noises, point at me, scratch themselves. They'd act like monkeys whenever they saw me, because I was one.

Debbi was already grinning and hooting, pretending to scratch under her arms. She stopped when Sandy defended me. *She didn't know,* Sandy said. Debbi said, *So what, she stepped right in it.* Sandy repeated, *She didn't know,* and Karen said, reluctantly, *You're right, it isn't fair.* Debbi sighed. She said, *Well, she can just jump it, then.* If you jumped the whole monkey box, you turned yourself back into a person. They showed me how far to back up, told me how fast to run, how to take off and land.

I backed up. I ran. I jumped. I landed.

Debbi said my heel touched the line. Karen said she wasn't sure.
Sandy said I made it without touching, and besides, I hadn't
known about it in the first place. A thing was fair, or it was not
fair. A thing was wrong or it was right. Your foot was in or it
was out. Or it was on the line. You could take it over sometimes,
if the judges were merciful. Debbi relented, although I could tell
she was disappointed.

Three years later I jumped ahead of them into the class of Sandy and
Karen's older sisters, skipping fourth grade. My fingers still smelled
of crayon, my left hand was still smeared with pencil lead. Sandy
and Karen forgot about me. Debbi forgot about me. But every
time I step around a monkey box, I remember them. Everything
straight-edged, the letters cut just so into the concrete.

Mirror in the Gym

Still panting from basketball and from
struggling into panty hose, miniskirts, bras,
we stand in a crowd and, if our hair is curly,
comb straight the damp strands tendriled
by sweat and shower mist, try to smooth
the kinks and frizzy ends. If our hair's straight
we rat it, and with the tail of the comb
try to lift it so it won't look flat. The hiss
of hairspray, our shrill voices, toilets flushing, steamy air
scented with Right Guard and cigarettes. Everybody wants to be
blond. Everybody wants to be tan. Everybody
wants to be beautiful. We flick mascara wands,
we rouge heat-pinked cheeks, we daub
cover-up on little red zits,
we lipstick perfect lips, our eyes
fixed on the mirror, trying to see
who we are, which face, where.

Household Blood

Having felt heavy for days, I feel it
rise like a dark river, broad and smooth,
murmuring in the shallows, full of
snags and eddies and hidden sandbars
and the faces of dead children.
For many nights I dream I walk its banks
picking among the litter, looking for something I need.
I meet my mother there.
Clean up this mess, she says,
and we embrace.

The Discovery of Sex

We try to be discreet standing in the dark
hallway by the front door. He gets his hands
up inside the front of my shirt and I put mine
down inside the back of his jeans. We are crazy
for skin, each other's skin, warm silky skin.
Our tongues are in each other's mouths,
where they belong, home at last. At first

we hope my mother won't see us, but later we don't care,
we forget her. Suddenly she makes a noise
like a game show alarm and says *Hey! Stop that!*
and we put our hands out where she can see them.
Our mouths stay pressed together, though, and
when she isn't looking anymore our hands go
back inside each other's clothes. We could

go where no one can see us, but we are
good kids, from good families, trying to have
as much discreet sex as possible with my mother and father
four feet away watching strangers kiss on TV,
my mother and father who once did as we are doing,
something we can't imagine because we know

that before we put our mouths together, before
the back seat of his parents' car where our skins
finally become one—before us, these things
were unknown! Our parents look on in disbelief
as we pioneer delights they thought only they knew
before those delights gave them us.

Years later, still we try to be discreet, standing
in the kitchen now where we think she can't see us. I
slip my hands down inside the back of his jeans
and he gets his up under the front of my shirt.
We open our mouths to kiss and suddenly *Hey! Hey!*
says our daughter glaring from the kitchen doorway.
Get a room! she says, as we put our hands
out where she can see them.

Second Decade

A person doesn't have to be bigger than you are to be bigger than you are.
Laura Willett draws in minutes what it takes me days to write.
Boys will never like me as much as they like Arlene Hall.
The wrong dress is like a bloody wound among chickens.
Nothing is more humiliating than eating lunch alone.
Sometimes the smartest girls get the worst grades.
What you write can make people remember you.
Even when you get A's, grades depress you.
Goodness can be very boring.
Brett Stark is worth it.
Even I can be cruel.

I used to be in love with Gretchen Miller.
Chris Pundeff's mind is like the cave of Ali Baba.
In the music room, it doesn't matter what you wear.
Monica Kish has more courage than a thousand guidance counselors.
Nothing makes holes in marshmallows like a parabolic mirror on a sunny day.
The essence of an entire year can live in four measures of a song.
Bach can get all thirty-five of us off the ground at the same time.
Nothing is more humiliating than a zit.
Bob Wells's ideas give me goosebumps.
Not even my father can teach me math.
I think I'd do anything for Chris Ness.

The most important thing about college is your mother's not there.
When they're older than you are, they look like they really know.
Professors do not give a flying fuck how clean your room is.
Dorm life only exacerbates the great sock mystery.
Hormones are stronger than homework.
Sex really is everything they say it is.
After the abortion, the baby stays with you.
When you can eat whatever you want, you do.
After the first psychedelic, the world looks different.
Nothing is more humiliating than your own ignorance.
If you're not paying attention, you won't even notice Jim Rolens.

Snow

The first time I was in real snow, it was Christmas
in Boulder, Colorado, after a long separation
from my first love. I remember the shock of his body
when I touched him again, the smell of him
once so familiar and now like a dream remembered.
He had grown taller, his arms harder, rounder
under their still-soft skin. The taste of his mouth
had the strangeness of homecoming. His hair was short,
his laugh was loud, his conversation easy—I'd missed him
as though he'd died, and now here he was,
alive as though he'd been living all along.
We walked down the frozen streets, my shoes so thin
my feet were as cold as death. He wore
ski clothes, warm boots. He hardly felt the cold, he said,
and I believed him. When the snow came down
he thought it beautiful. He thought me beautiful.
I couldn't get enough of him, of his skin
so hot beneath his clothes it hurt my hands to touch him.
He could live in any weather. I was shocked
at the blatant cold, the blandness of the winter sky,
the impersonal flakes that puzzled my eyes, each
so carefully designed to fall at random.
So cold. I didn't know how heavy and deep it can get,
how it freezes the blood and makes the road deadly,
how it falls in confusion everywhere you look
until you see only cold chaos, obscuring everything.

Jackpot in My Pocket

Another House for Peace

One Saturday a southern storm made the walls sweat from basement to attic. Too humid to do homework or watch the Vietnam War on TV. At noon Constantine pulled off his T-shirt and went to find someone to sleep with. Celeste made blackberry jam in the kitchen, Robby ate it on Lynne's homemade bread, Adriana washed the dishes. Sun contemplated her right to kill ants, as a trail of the tiny beings headed for the tofu. Warner described what ant poison does to the environment. Cindy theorized about barometric pressure, which Rik compared to a summer's day.

At four twenty I opened the pantry door. All the labels had come loose from the cans and lay curled in delicate heaps on the floor. I took up a can I thought might be corn. From its shiny surface a small face stared back at me and said, *What was tuna might now be pineapple. What was peaches might now be refried beans. In a true democracy, how impossible it is to know the future!*

A Waltz

Reluctantly the boys lugged the stereo
out onto the terrace where we could
smell the honeysuckle. Do we have to
dress up? they asked. Do we have to dance,
or can we just watch? Where's the food?
Some of us could dance. Joan knew the grapevine,
Cindy could tango, Celeste did a snaky slink
like Lauren Bacall in *To Have and Have Not*.
The boys tried a few turns, stepped on everyone's feet,
begged off. They were small men, good-looking,
but they moved like large herbivorous dinosaurs
and preferred aiming champagne corks
out over the stone wall. Only Neil wanted to dance,
all three hundred pounds of him, dressed
in a faded tuxedo. Red-faced, breathless,
he appraised us as we leaned in our long gowns
against the brick barbecue. Joan put on a waltz,
grabbed Dave, twirled him onto the flagstones.
Neil offered me his hand. He danced

the way Picasso might have sketched
on an envelope at the *Lapin Agile*,
or as Beethoven might have whistled
walking through the woods. Our feet
stayed on the ground but our bodies
spun above the flagstones. I danced two dances
clinging to his soft bulk, my body doing exactly
what he wanted. Then I leaned against the bricks
and watched him dance one by one with the others,
his white shirt gleaming, flashing as he turned,

his feet never faltering, always near his partner's
but never touching, his face placid, confident.
I watched carefully, trying to see how he did it,
how a three-hundred-pound man became as weightless
as the scent of honeysuckle on the warm night air.

Gallo

The year Dr. King died, and Bobby Kennedy, the year of the
Chicago Seven, we took a jug of Gallo to the quarry, Jim, Tom,
Nancy and me, four brand-new freshmen. It was dark, it was
late, we were drunk and laughing. It was before Richard Nixon,
before People's Park, before the draft lottery, before Kent State
and the bombing of Cambodia.

We could have drunk the Gallo in the dorm, hidden under loud
music. Hendrix was still alive, and Jim Morrison, and Janis.
The Beatles were still together. Tom hadn't been arrested yet,
Jim hadn't failed the core course. Nancy hadn't sailed away on a
boat with her fourth boyfriend and a St. Bernard called Leroy.
But we left the dorm, took our Gallo to the quarry, sat on the
steps at the very bottom, and drank.

Then Tom kissed Nancy.

I watched him do it, with the empty redwood forest stirring
around us, all the stars out, no grownups for miles. It happened
in regular motion but I saw it slowly, what was now possible.
We passed Tom the jug and he gave it to Nancy, and after she
drank he kissed her again. Jim took the jug and drank and
passed it to me. Nancy kissed Jim, and then after I drank, Tom
kissed me. Nobody was gentle. We were drunk, it was late.
When Tom kissed Nancy again, Jim kissed me.

He did it with abandon, with thoroughness. What kissing is
when a boy treats you as though you are both made of the same
tough material.

Not romantic. Just a pure thrill, like driving fast, like putting
your toes on purpose on the edge of a cliff, knowing you could fall.

Pearl Divers

I have read about Japanese pearl divers,

plump women in white robes
who glide obliquely through cold salt water,

women who can hold their breaths a full minute
or more, as they part the seaweed.
When they enter the water, they know

what to look for. Wordless, full of intent,
they enter my mind,

where I see them
the way they see the pearl.

Castle Beach

Two months before we first sleep together I go down
to watch Jim swim in the sea. Tom comes too. Tom and I
split a hit of some psychedelic whose name I don't know.
We sit on the sand. Jim, cold sober, takes off his clothes,
goes into the water in his warm pink skin, comes out
shaking, unable to speak. He lies in the sun trembling,
purple with cold, his long blond hair in the sand. What
a stud, says Tom. What a mighty Viking. Jim

shivers and shivers in his suit of goosebumps while I
marvel at the beauty of the sand, its tiny
multicolored pebbles all the same size each
perfectly rounded so minute so exquisite!
And look, I can hold them in my hand!

Two Students

It was a new Random House, the College Edition, with a little drawing of a house on the title page. He kept it on a shelf beside his bed. Sprawled on the pale green sheets, we started with *penis* from the Latin for *tail*, which was near *penitence* from the Latin for *regretting*. *Vagary* from the Latin for *to wander* came before *vagina* from the Latin for *sheath*. *Orgasm* was from the Greek *orgasmos*, "excitement," from *orgaein*, "to swell." *Testicles* came from *testis*, "gonad," and nearby, *testify*, from *testis*, "witness." *Ovary* led to *ovation*, "a triumph," and *ovate*, all from *ovum*, Latin for *egg*. *Clitoris*, from the Greek for *to shut*, had on either side *Clisthenes* ("poor guy," he said) and *Clive, Robert*. *Coleridge* came just before *coleslaw*. *Sex* meant "either male or female" or "the instinct drawing one individual to another" or "to ascertain the gender of newly hatched chicks."

The dictionary had thumb tabs cut in the pages for every two letters of the alphabet. Inside the front, his mother had written his last name in her distinctive hand. He had folded a cover for the dictionary out of a brown paper bag. When the book lay open on the blanket it was heavy and hard to push aside, and would sometimes slip to the floor with a startling thud.

Later we moved on to *freedom*, "the state of being at liberty," and *liberty*, "independence," and *independence*, "exemption from outside influence or control." We looked up *equality*, "the state of being equal," and *equal*, "of the same in quantity, degree, or merit: two students of equal brilliance."

Mary Guilfoyle
in memoriam

1.

It was like living inside a corpse, that house on Clay Street our
landlord Frank bought when the old man died—battered siding,
mildewed contents coated with ancient dust. He didn't clean it,
just rented it out to us, dirty dishes still in the sink, termite frass,
crumbling plaster sifting down. I could stick my finger through
wood and it splintered like old bone. Moldy carpets, ribboned
wallpaper, all the floors tilted, no drawers stayed shut, we had to
open the slope-shouldered fridge with Greg's screwdriver. Had water
fights in the kitchen, and once Margaret brought home day-old pies
for us to throw. Rain dripped into the silverware drawer, Martha
made dinner, Greg would say come eat in the bosom of your family.

2.

But at two in the morning the smell of the old man's skin would rise
up from the mattress through my thin sheets. What was I doing
with my life? I put my feet to the gritty floor, moved through the
brooding house, the subtle breathing, out past the jasmine. Lay
down under the apricot tree, heard drunks, drug dealers, Vietnam
vets singing in the dark.

3.

Or walked all hours along the levee, alone with the smell of river
mud, wild dill, dry weeds, ducks, the sea. I had just gotten my
bachelor's degree, was washing dishes for new freshmen. Went to
weekend parties on the west side, poker games downtown, walked
home alone along the levee way past midnight, tequila buzz, a jackpot
in my pocket, my hair long and loose, saw the moon on the river,
listened to the sea roar like the Dead, like twenty thousand peace
marchers. The smell of dill along the levee, the air like brine. I
walked to Jim's above the rivermouth with nothing on under my
skirt to see what he'd do, watched ducks glide, seagulls with shellfish
flesh dangling from their beaks swoop above the roller coaster, pelicans
wheeling above the waves, salt wind in my face.

4.

And sometimes stuck out my thumb if I got tired of walking.
They took me into their cars, offered me hits of weed, sips of beer,
old clothes from the back seat, bags of apples and tomatoes, what
they thought of Nixon, Reagan, Jesus, young girls who hitchhiked.
Weed should be legal, acid should be legal. I should get on with
my life. Some said did I ever think I might experiment with—
No? Oh well. They were big, little, women, men, long hair, short
hair, flash cars, coughing old jalopies, milk trucks, an old bus,
expounding their faith in God or the latest conspiracy theory. And
did I think his pants were too tight? Just let me off here, I'd say, I
can walk home from here.

5.

Until the afternoon Greg sat reading the *Sentinel* over coffee before
his shift, Margaret baking bread, Martha typing her thesis in the
kitchen, me trying to write but choked by the smell of the house,
the cabinets angled like Dr. Caligari, the walls always damp, the
faucet dripping. Margaret tipped out her bread fresh from the
oven, I gripped my pen, Martha typed her final word, and Greg
read to us about a girl's severed head found by hikers in the woods,
too decomposed for immediate identification, only her long hair
unchanged.

Every Word

1. Geraniums
I walk down the path that winds
past beds of geraniums,
the first flower I know by name.
My mother works among them,
her hands and the leaves
giving off a spicy scent.

Out in the street the big boys fly
small balsa-wood airplanes. I want to fly one too,
but when I throw one it crashes head-first
onto the asphalt. The boys don't like this.
Go away, they say, but that makes me cry.
Stand here, one says finally, *and watch how I do it.*
I stand where he tells me, and he goes a little way,
flings the small plane into the air, and it
banks suddenly, heads straight for me
and smacks me in the head. I hear the loud
thud as the metal tip meets my temple.

I am lying quietly in a bed of crushed flowers,
their scent rising around me without a word.

2. Horse
The center of this is walking the horses back. Big white clouds
in a blue sky. Beige stucco buildings. Too many cars, the sun
glinting off their windows. Everything swirls around me.
The sound of a stream, for instance. The ground
coming toward me. A loud thump. Trees. The smell
of sagebrush and water. The white horse has too broad a back,
a cockeyed canter. The other girls laugh at first. Trees.
The ground is hard. The first horse, the bay,
has a spine like a saw-blade. I beg to trade. Or are we

walking the horses back? I fall from the white horse,
big white clouds in a blue sky. I reach for my name
but it's gone. So's my phone number
(they have to look it up, their lips twitching).

I grope through my head, searching. A loud
thump. When I come to, they're standing over me
trying not to laugh. The white horse moves too fast,
he's too fat, I can't get a grip with my knees. *At least she knows
she doesn't know*, the white-coated man at the hospital
tells my father. *That only happens
to the smart ones*. The ground moves up fast.

3. Mescaline
Five in the morning, the drug still in me,
I wake up wordless, my mind wiped clean slick sweaty
against hard into fragrant spicy with a
white mildly curious. Panicky!
Dark blank empty!

Nothing has a name. When I calm down
I feel lighter, a burden lifted. I glide easily,
no heavy between me and falling
my skin uninterpreted, the floor bare
the soft breezy, the hard cold open.

A blue flower springs from the top
of white metal in the best-smelling room.
From the side of curved silver with two-holed top
a bent face looks back. What to call the face?
Who is this? No way to ask. I go back to bed
and to sleep, still not knowing.

Moment of Inertia

It's what makes the pancake hold still
while you slip the spatula under it
so fast it doesn't move, my father said
standing by the stove.

All motion stopped when he died.
With his last breath the earth
lurched to a halt and hung still on its axis,
the atoms in the air
coming to rest within their molecules,
and in that moment
something slid beneath me
so fast I couldn't move.

Petit Mal

The light is there. The light
is not there. He loves me, he loves me
not, strobing the sun with splayed
fingers like the spokes of a wheel. *Did you
hear what I just said?* I hear.
I don't hear. They say I never listen.
The world's there, the world's
not there, and when it returns everybody's
laughing. *Your name was called,* they say.
Why weren't you listening?

I read black words on the white page. I read fast, faster,
the page blurs grey and is gone. Then
it returns. I look around
to see if anybody saw.

On a boulevard lined with trees
the sun flashes in and out as we drive by.
Black or white? Yes or no?
How serene the surface of a plain grey road.
Hot or cold? Right or left?
I choose: I choose not to.

The computer flickers. If it all goes away
I just wait for the next frame. If they want an answer
they'll ask again, or they'll stop asking. The world
will return. Light shines steadily
through the open window.

Painting Houses

You had to prepare the surface first,
scrape down to bare wood
so the new paint would lie smooth.
You had to lay drop cloths, had to
mask the glass, and only then
open the can and gently stir the paint.

Never dip the brush in all the way at first,
he said, just wet the end, just rest it
against the lip of the can, the paint like
liquid silk, pleasant between fingers,
skin rubbing paint rubbing skin.

He was faster and more expert,
I was slower and more dreamy,
prone to fantasize while moving
the brush delicately along the sash,
near the glass but never touching.
He did the muscle work, rolling
walls and ceilings, sweat and paint
in his eyes, ready for a cigarette
at the end of each hour. I took care
of the subtleties, though he could be
subtle too, drawing his brush
deftly along smooth surfaces.

At the end of the day, we moved
tentatively through the painted rooms,
careful not to stir up dust, not to touch
wet paint, and when we met
stood still a moment, hands in our pockets,
only our mouths touching.

French Kissing

How can you talk about that
at a time like this? my sister-in-law said
at my father's funeral. It was afterward,
we were outside, my brother smoking, his mouth
making that tiny *tsup* when he sucked in smoke,
just like my father. *Why not?* my brother said,
and we laughed, we were so tired of crying.
What do they call it in France? my sister asked,
and we laughed some more, smoke
shooting out my brother's nose.

My father used to smoke outside the bedroom
where he died (his last breaths
minutes apart) or out
in the side yard under a smog-yellow sky
while our mother sat in the house
watching television. Our father
would look in through the window at her
while he stood smoking, smoking.

Suddenly our mother is with us,
our father's wedding ring around
her neck on a chain, the ring she removed
so tenderly from his dead finger. My brother
puts out his cigarette. *French kissing?* she says,
her eyes red-rimmed. *Ugh! Disgusting!*
How could anyone stand it? she says, pretending
to spit out something unpleasant.

Bathroom Mirror after Midnight

Because I never turn on the light
my face, shapeless in the mirror,
darker than the reflected dark,
makes me think of the dead I know,
my cousins, my grandparents,
my father whose dead face I kissed
as willingly as when he was alive.
I turn away quickly, go back to bed
where I feel as though I hold my father again,
his head in the hollow of my arms.

Clarence

When I knew him he was thirty, six foot six, dark as a Masai warrior. As school custodian he made coffee, cleaned rooms, moved furniture, made sure AJ Rodriguez and Marcus Washington didn't fight or leave school before three o'clock, shot hoops with the kids, even the girls. He pruned roses, raked leaves, cut grass, made sets for the school play, gave speeches to the boys about bathroom accuracy.

Clarence drove a white Continental Mark IV, the biggest car in the parking lot. He owned a tank of tropical fish. One day he took his fish for a ride in his Continental. *Wanted to give 'em some fun*, he said. He drove them three times around the block. *Half of 'em died the next day*, he said, *but they died happy*.

His favorite ride in the Continental had been with a friend after drinking a fifth of scotch. They cruised along the canal road by the railroad tracks. It was spring, the fragrance of new-mown hay in the air. For no good reason Clarence made a sharp right turn and the car became airborne, sailing over the canal. I imagine it jumping clear of its accustomed medium, like the shark at the end of *Jaws*. When it came to rest, undamaged, Clarence and his friend sat still inside it for a moment, savoring the memory of their flight. Then they got out and walked home.

Clarence believed the local Chinese restaurant served cats and dogs in their mu shu and stir fry. People's pets disappeared, he said. *Can't keep no cats and dogs when you live near China Alley*, he said. *I don't eat nothin' but vegetables there. They prices so low, can't be nothin' but cats and dogs they servin'*. At the end of the school year we had a lunch at the China Cafe for our retiring principal, the whole staff at one long table in the seedy upstairs room, Clarence a little way down from where I sat. When the food arrived, the principal made a speech and gave a toast. As we reached for our glasses, Clarence caught my eye. He pointed to my food, smiled gravely, put a finger beside his nose. I raised my glass to him. I raise it now.

Rhythm of the Blood

Pomegranate

Open it—
an ancient queen's tomb
filled with edible rubies,
opulent, astringent,
with seeds like small teeth
or bits of old soft bone.

The rubies nestle
hexagonally
like honeycomb
or catacomb.

I eat flesh and seeds,
sweet with bitter,
peeling away
the pale membrane.

See how the light glints, even now,
on the red gems, and see
how delicately the mold
clings along the edge
of the catacomb.

Giving Birth

for my daughter

The small
damp-haired skull
split my flesh,
her wet skin
warm and slithery
against my belly,
her fists waving.
Her cry, a real baby's,
shocked me more
than if I had brought
spices to the tomb, seen
the stone rolled away,
seen the bloody linen
and the angel.

Cow

When the first mouth closed around my nipple
I felt a twinge between my legs, but I took no notice.
Later, when I began to croon deep in my chest,
I could feel the bony sockets stand out above my eyes.
Slowly I realized
that I smelled of milk and got restless at certain hours,
that as my breasts grew tight and heavy
my hip bones jutted up when I lay down
and my hunger was like an empty barn.
The more my young bleated and rubbed against my legs
the more my jaw tightened, eager for some kind of rhythm,
the more I wanted just to wade out into the clover
and watch mindless insects climb up the fairy antlers,
the more inviting I thought the Charolais
with his smooth white skin drawn tight
over the twitching muscles of his haunches.

July Twenty-first
1983, 1987

My father's glasses lie by the bed. I watch his eyes. *In labor I leaned against the wall, breathed fast, in out, in out, until the pain passed. In the mirror I saw the world before my daughter.* My father wants water but sucks ice, breathes slowly in, out. I smash ice for him on the kitchen sink. *I wanted water but sucked ice, pressed my palms flat against the wallpaper, kept my eyes on one scrolled rose. My glasses lay by the bed.*

My father says he feels no pain, asks for water, sucks ice. My mother and my sister rub his feet, cool his brow, murmur to him. He breathes slowly, his eyes fixed on a spot high on the wall. *In labor I sucked ice, breathed rapidly, my eyes on the rose. I felt my daughter kick inside me.* My father is nothing but sallow skin draped over bones, death kicking against every breath, his breathing slow now, slower. He asks for water. He needs air but gets ice, while the nurse listens to his heart. It beats fast, faster. *I was round and sleek, flushed and panting. The nurse listened to my daughter's heart. I saw my eyes in the mirror round with pain.* My father breathes slowly in, slowly out. He asks for water. The nurse lets him drink.

The doctor reached cold metal up inside me, fit the forceps around my daughter's head. The pain stopped my breath, and the nurse listened in vain for my daughter's heart. Now my sister cries out, and my mother, and the nurse shouts Come quick! *Breathe! the doctor shouted, and my daughter's heart beat again.* The nurse listens for my father's heart, which has beat all my life. His eyes are closed. *My daughter was pulled from me and took her first breath and cried out.* My father breathes one long, slow breath, and is pulled from us without a sound.

Now we sit at the kitchen table sobbing. I lay my glasses down. *When we took my daughter home I put my glasses on. I looked and looked at my daughter, at her smooth new face, her eyes my father's eyes.* I lift my daughter up and she lays her cheek against my heart. I put my glasses on. I look in the mirror and see the world without my father. My heart beats against the bones of my face. I breathe slowly in. Out.

Day Bath

for my son

Last night I walked him back and forth,
his small head heavy against my chest,
round eyes watching me in the dark,
his body a sandbag in my arms.
I longed for sleep but couldn't bear his crying
so bore him back and forth until the sun rose
and he slept. Now the doors are open,
noon sunlight coming in,
and I can see fuchsias opening.
Now we bathe. I hold him, the soap
makes our skins glide past each other.
I lay him wet on my thighs, his head on my knees,
his feet dancing against my chest,
and I rinse him, pouring water
from my cupped hand.
No matter how I feel, he's the same,
eyes expectant, mouth ready,
with his fat legs and arms,
his belly, his small solid back.
Last night I wanted nothing more
than to get him out of my arms.
Today he fits neatly
along the hollow my thighs make,
and with his fragrant skin against mine
I feel brash, like a sunflower.

Clay's House

When I can't sleep I think of it,
four plain rooms with smooth silent walls.

In the afternoon I walk by with my children.
The sound of Clay's piano swells, grows louder,
then fades as we go past on our way toward town.

When his music fills the rooms and floats
out the screen door onto the tangled roses,
the sound moves through his house as through a shell.

All day my children's voices fill my ears,
my head still ringing after they are still.

At night when Clay lies thinking before he sleeps,
his head echoes only the sound of his four rooms.

When I can't sleep I think of it,
those four plain rooms that hold no sound but his.

Menstruation for Men

Find a blood plum, the kind that grow along the Amazon
where the jungle reaches right down to the water's edge,
no land to set your foot on, just fluid vines and water.
The blood plum has thick red flesh under skin so thin
it splits at a touch, thick juice a feral smell on the fingers.

Take off your clothes and put the blood plum
between the tops of your thighs. Find something
to keep the juice off your clothes. Then get dressed.

Now leave for work. You may be amazed just how much liquid
a blood plum holds, but walk normally. Behave normally,
even when juice from the plum leaks out onto your skin,
or when you feel pieces of plum flesh detach from the pit.
No one must know. Not strangers, not your boss, not blood
relatives, not the checker at the market. When you have a headache,
or your lower back hurts, or you feel bloated, light-headed,
can't think straight, suddenly feel like crying,
then sometimes you can tell your best friend. But don't
go on about it. It happens to all of us, no big deal.
Sit in the important meeting waiting to make your presentation
on a new marketing strategy for the quick fix, and don't think
about what might happen if you stand up too fast. After work,

on the sidewalk waiting for a green light,
concrete and steel rising all around you, car exhaust,
humanity dense as undergrowth, notice you can still feel
the jungle tendrils creeping between your thighs, feel the strong
liquid pulse of the wild broad river, hear the beat of it in your ears,
smell in your nostrils the feral scent of your own bright blood.

In Flanders Fields

In spring the Iceland poppies
hang their buds, firm little spheres,
each seamed like a fig, each bud
covered with tiny fur
erect and sharp to the touch,

just as the two small orbs
in their little stippled sac
nestle between men's thighs
like warm soft fruit. There hangs

our human future, guarded only
by shoulders and legs,
strong arms. How delicate

the skin of the little sac is, how
tenderly the whole thing sits in the hand,
one rough touch a torture. No wonder

men and boys all seem to know
about guns and swords, how to make
the sound, at least, of every weapon.

In Arles

for Lin Rolens

For just two thousand dollars we could buy a house
in Arles, where Van Gogh lived.
You can't smell the sea in Arles, and there is no work.
The autumn windfalls are green and bitter,
and snow on stubble fields kills the winter air.
But the buds don't know this, and in spring
the uninformed orchards still turn out snowy hearts.
Above wheatfields the summer sun always spreads its petals.

Van Gogh sketched the harvest
and penciled in color names so his brush would know.
Houses resting among wheatfields told him their hues in all seasons.

There is always a chance of a yellow house with spare, clean rooms,
a garden where blue iris thrust straight up,
where the mind is swept clean
by the arc of a sudden
flight of birds.

Lascaux

In spring we lie out at the edge of the plain,
feel the thud of hoofs through the ground
near our hearts. Breath hanging in clouds,
flint points flaked sharp, we wait. The bulls
have warm flanks and thick fur,
they snort and spar, they lick each other
with rough tongues, and the mothers
nuzzle their young. To capture a perfect bull,
to kill him beautifully, this
is what we wait for.

In winter no herds, no hunt. We wait
by the fire where the cave roof smokes and curves like the sky.
Above a shelf of rock we see a bull lift his head, see a bear
hump up from a hard curve, a horse's back
rise from solid rock. Deep snow outside, but in here a whole herd
gallops beneath a cumulus of stone along scalloped ridges. With
spit and ash we coax from folds of stone the branching
antlers, the dancing hoofs of deer. A running bull, eye closed,
swishes his tail. On the moonmilk-coated nave
a herd of charcoal deer move toward red bulls
on our stone altar. We love what feeds us,
what dies for life. Here we draw the drumming hoofs
and the sharp spear's flight, the bleeding bull, the taste
of flesh and blood. To capture a perfect bull, to draw him
beautifully, this is what we live for.

Washing

I still love to take them from the washing machine
and drop them in the wicker basket. They smell of soap,
sweet and hopeful, a harvest of damp clean clothes,
and I hang them on the line to dry.

My father used to wash us kids like cars. Our eyes
were headlights, our hands and feet were tires,
our butts the rumbleseats. His hands were big and square,
precise and graceful. *Now I wash the headlights,*
he'd say, *keep them closed!* while he held my head
in one square hand. *Now the grille work!*
There in the tub we could hardly stand for laughing.
Dry, we slipped between clean white sheets,
his big hands pulling up the covers.

As he lay dying he'd have only my mother
wash him. He followed her with his eyes,
running his gaze up and down her body,
too weak to smile. It was their love-making and their hope,
that somehow her touch could rescue his flesh, make him new.

When he died my mother washed him one last time
with water warmer than his skin, her hands caressing him,
washing away the pain. She washed him crying softly,
dried him, kissed him, covered him with a clean white sheet,
left the room and never looked back
at what he had become, as though all she needed
was to know his death by washing.

Afterward we washed his sheets, his last clothes,
pulled them up damp and fresh-smelling from the machine,
put them in the wicker basket,
hung them on the line
to dry in the wind.

Rembrandt's *The Raising of Lazarus*
for Fr. Lawrence K. Mikkelsen Jr.

I take this tomb's darkness to heart
because I expect to die and be held down
by this same blackness,
full of silence, deaf to grief.

I look for things that give back light,
that might point a way out—
those gilded scabbards, Lazarus' bloodless face,
the eager onlookers,
the gleam of Jesus' tears.

Above the crypt, Jesus
raises his arm and sees stunned Lazarus rise.
Something like wonder
rises in Jesus' face,
as though in Lazarus' quickened corpse
he sees an unexpected glint.

Feigning faith, I strain
to see what he sees,

and why, in light of it,
he weeps here on the crypt's edge,
arm and eyebrow raised,
lifting the darkness.

Feast of All Saints

Sometimes the sun shines, slanting through the trees
as we cross the grass beside the church. Sometimes
it rains, and inside we close our umbrellas,
hear on the roof the feet of the invisible host.

We begin with priest and acolytes
white-robed to the altar. We hear
a lesson from St. Jesus, son of Sirach, who bids us
consider past generations, praise famous men. We hear
from St. John, our cryptic from Patmos, and from
the gospel of Matthew, the saint who once collected
our taxes. We speak the psalm which says *Let us be
joyful on our beds.* We hear the homily. When the wind
rises, blowing dry leaves, we speak
the names of our dead.

Some go by placidly, some
bring sorrow that passes like wind
over grass. We remember the St. Thomases
More and Cranmer, St. Martin Luther King
martyred in Alabama, St. Oscar Romero
in El Salvador, St. Joan of Arc, St. Mary Magdalene,
St. Eleanor Roosevelt, St. Teresa of Calcutta,
the Blessed Virgin Mary. We speak

the name of St. Edie, the deep voice in the bell choir
who knew all the bawdy songs, St. Anneliese with the kind face,
St. Mary Mosby, whose great granddaughters are

still here, four generations in this parish. The St. Donalds
Anderson and Matchan, St. Alice who loved the stories
of Turgenev, St. Christina who, though young,
made a good death, full of love and humor. We remember

St. Lawrence our priest, who, ill, fell
still holding the chalice. We speak their names

singly and in family groups, every November, until we know
each other's dead—Michael's Louise, Charles's Mary Lou—
as friends never met. Rain falls. Sun shines. We speak
swaying as we listen, all swaying
in the same wind. We circle the altar
to receive the host, the wine from the chalice, and the dead
stand with us, swaying too, Joan and Thomas,
Mary and Donald, Lawrence and Edie and Anneliese,

saints in cowls, saints with bustles, saints in suits, saints
whose tongues we don't know but whose names we say
every November. We are the body of Christ, we hold
his body in our hands as the dead rustle among us
like rain or wind, and the host
spreads in our limbs like wine.

Paula and I Kill a Gopher

Let the righteous smite me; it shall be a kindness.
David, *Psalm 141*

Standing where ranunculus should have been, Paula picked up
the metal box-trap. I saw him writhing, pinned inside, and I
screamed, and Paula screamed and dropped the trap, and we
both ran. We saw the gopher squirming and we screamed
again, shifting from foot to foot, our backs against the fence.

The gopher made no sound, but we saw him struggling against
the neck wire, back feet jerking. Wind stirred, bending the
stems of the coreopsis. Bees buzzed through the iris and the
zinnias.

We called Jim, and Jim said, Whatever you do, don't drown it.
They can swim, and even when they're injured, they're strong,
too hard to hold down. You can hit it with a shovel, or you can
just leave it alone, or you can find a vicious dog or cat to finish
it off for you.

I said, Come and help us. But he said, I'm just as repulsed as
you are.

Paula thought we could smother it with a plastic bag, but
when we looked in her kitchen all she had were the kind you
put broccoli in. Paula said we'd see right through it. We
might as well use a shovel.

We looked at her shovels but the box-trap was narrow. She
didn't think we could get a shovel in there, unless to bisect the
body lengthwise. I wanted to leave, just walk away, say, It's
your gopher. I thought of its bloody fur, its eyes.

We drifted around Paula's back yard hoping some humane weapon would come to hand, or Paula's Buddhist husband would come out and kill it, or Jim—once bitten by a gopher while setting a trap in its run—would have a change of heart.

After fretting among the ranunculus, we went for a walk.

Two in the City

1. *Les Miserables*
In front of the theatre the beggars
put out their hands. One walked beside me
and said, "You know, last week
I saw my mother riding down the street
in a limousine. She rolled down the window
and I saw her diamond ring. She was
so beautiful." He smelled bad, his skin was grey,
his jeans looked stiff and shiny. I had to go in
to meet someone at the Grand Cafe,
where I paid seven dollars for a glass of wine.
When my friend and I left, the same beggar
found me. I gave him two dollars
though he hadn't asked yet. He said,
"I saw my mother again the other day
in the lobby of the Mark. She was walking
with her escort of United States Marines,
so many people crowded around her! She wore
a mink coat and a tiara. When she passed me
she didn't see me, even though her fur brushed my hand."
I fingered two fives in my pocket. It was a warm night,
and I went into the theatre.

2. Near Union Square
In a crush of people I waited for the light
at Powell and Ellis. A beggar loomed up,
dark-skinned, young, good-looking, and held out
a giant palm. "Ma'am, could you spare . . ."
He watched me rummage in my pocket.
"Oh, you're gorgeous," he said, "you know that, right?
You're so gorgeous, absolutely gorgeous, I've never seen
anyone so gorgeous in my life." I laughed, hoping
no one around us heard, wondering why my heart
leapt when he said it. I handed him a dollar. "You *know*
you're gorgeous, don't you?" he said, and elbowed me
gently in the ribs. The light changed, I crossed the street,
and he called from the curb, "Gorgeous!"

Panties in the Street

Black lace rolled into a figure eight
at the edge of the sidewalk, lavender spandex
wadded tightly in the gutter, pink cotton
draped on a bus-stop bench along the boulevard.
On a wire fence down a back alley, on a quiet
street near the library, a single pair swept aside
by the wheels of a passing car, alone
or with a wrinkled condom nearby
like the shed skin of a snake, panties
delicate, abandoned, flaming red or cool blue
or ice white against the blacktop. They fell

from the top of the laundry bag
while she struggled to hold the kids' hands
crossing the street. He threw them out
of the car after he dropped her off, not wanting
to leave them for his wife to find. His
blunt-fingered hands jerked them off
or her own small trembling hands
rolled them down her thighs, her eyes

on the gun or the knife. They were both middle-aged,
so drunk such niceties as panties no longer mattered,
didn't even glance around for the cops
out here under what stars still shine
through a city night, out here among
the bourgeoisie and the Republicans.
They were in their late teens or early
twenties walking home toward parents
or roommates, prurience more urgent
with every step. They were stoned or maybe

just sick of being good, the trap of school
or jobs looming ahead of them, they
shucked off prudence as quickly as the panties,
a hand up under her skirt, a furtive
glance up and down the dark deserted street,
hearts beating, the first of many heedless acts,
or the last daring thing they'd ever do.

Chivalry

He strolls down the middle of the sidewalk
leaving little room for me. I lag behind
to get around an open gate, to avoid
a fence post, a mailbox sticking out.
You don't walk as fast as you used to, he says,
striding ahead on his personal red carpet,
feet turned slightly out, a spring in his step
like he's about to go up for a jump shot.
I dodge a low branch and the open door
of a parked car. Just as I decide
to hip-check him out into the street
he stops and crouches to pet
a little white cat. He croons to her,
stroking her arched back. The cat
closes her eyes and I think of how he sleeps
nestled against me, turning when I turn
all night long, and never wakes me.

Collecting

The roadkill snakes lie flat as prey
on the bookcase, their skulls
tiny arrowheads, one jagged jaw
crushed open in a silent cry. Nearby

crouches the hollow squash, round
as a baby's head, its insides dried
to weightlessness. A breeze
stirs dust-curls on the skeleton
that hangs on the wall, once lifted whole
from the cooked flesh of a fish. From its spine
filaments of white ribs climb
like beansprouts, pale bones freed
from muscle and blood. Here's the small skull
brought up from the beach, blunt-nosed and bleached,
stained pink where flesh touched the grooved
surface of bone. It waits among shells, leaves,
rocks, the blown eggs of unfledged birds, and its eyes,
shrunk to wrinkled olives in black sockets, move
as I move. On the right midnight the skull will lift
its upper jaw, stinking like a thing long dead,
and cry with the voice of the sea. Then

dead snakes will slither, each in its own wandering
S, the round squash roll, the shells extend their legs
and walk again, the dead leaves swirl, the blown eggs
hatch, and the rocks—dark agate like congealed blood,
strong hunks of granite, obsidian spiked like
shards of glass, sandstone bearing the fossil teeth
of sharks—the rocks too will rise,
rocks, which never die.

Jack O'Lantern

Even on a moonless night I know these streets,
the old hitching post by the Windham Market,
this cottage behind the picket fence, the yard
with beds full of chard and the skeletons of peas,
the bare persimmon tree where the hard fruit
hang like human hearts. Lights from pumpkins
glow like windows of houses. A drowned man
walks with a pirate, a corpse on the executioner's heels,
Madonna arm in arm with Carmen Miranda, and then
the four feathered dancehall girls, who, when asked,
dance here on Windham in the streetlight
and then move on. It is a warm night.
Seeds sleep uneasily, unsure of their time,
poised to sprout but wary of the cold,
of the old year dying but not dead.
All along the dark streets, bands
of little goblins pass, carrying their burdens,
traveling by foot as in the old days,
and under the black moon years slide away.

Up on Frederick Street a throng of creatures
parades from parish hall to church.
Skeleton, panther, country bumpkin, a dead
bridesmaid on the arm of James Dean.
Albert Einstein and Groucho Marx stroll past
as the groundfog thickens. Shriners in fezzes
ride by in their calliope truck. I hear the bagpipe band, I turn
and there they are, stepping solemnly, kilts swaying.
The sixth grade girl I saw today above the dunk tank
walks by. I see her plunge into the chilly water,
her startled face among the churning bubbles,
wet hair like seaweed, arms
flailing like drowning. She passes me
as though I'm not here, and in the distance

up the block on Windsor, over on Pine,
down Ocean View, I see them all
moving in little groups, little
gleams of light—gypsy, warrior,
angel, king.

In the middle of the carnival
walk the dead, numerous as the living,
and if they speak tonight, we will hear them.
I listen for those who carry in clutched hands
some dim light. Doomed to walk the earth,
the legends say, to roam the roads
and meadows under moonlight, the glistening
rounded hills, the creeks where the smell
of water and rocks rises up. Doomed
to watch fairy lanterns, columbine, trillium,
forget-me-nots bloom again and again,
doomed to watch the sun rise and set, to hear
the wind blow, to see the block of lamplight fall
along the lawn from the open door.

On Windham between Pine and Caledonia the four
dancehall girls return, feather boas, black stockings,
high heels. They dance again there in the street,
kicking their legs in unison, then walk on
until they're a block away on Windsor,
and then three blocks off on Cayuga
clinging to each other, giggling.

Porch lights out now, the pumpkin houses
silent under the poplars. Tonight
I'd give up sleep, hunger, lust, hope,
the rhythm of blood beating in the veins,
just to walk here forever, a vegetable lamp
with a coal from hell to light my way.

Songs in Every Tongue

Listening to Irish Pipes

The stone walls are a drone
through the green idle fields, a drone
like an owl's tuneless song.
And a man sings in a tongue
shaped by hunger, by the way
the hungry breathe while dancing,
by the way wind comes off the sea
and bumps into low hills
and blows, and blows, and bumps
into more low hills and then
blows back out to sea.

The man sings above
the bodhran, the drum beaten
with the same motion as dough
so that when there is no bread
he may still sing
on his stony, windy ground
that never will sustain him,
where he stays, and sings, and burns
and breathes the blue peat smoke
and blows out a song to the drone
like dry stone walls that move
through the green and barren fields.

The News from Dublin

Margaret Mulrooney sits with her son's fiancee from America watching a movie on the telly, when Clint Eastwood comes squinting onto the screen. Margaret says, *I heard he's the son of Stan Laurel—you know, the thin one who goes with the fat one, and he with the little hat. Stan Laurel! And doesn't he look like him though. And they have the same hair.*

Her son's fiancee, my sister, doesn't laugh at first, only turns to her future mother-in-law. *Say that again, please*, she says. When Margaret says it again her husband Jimmy comes in. *I'm after hearing that down at the pub*, he says, *and I believe it. Look at the face on him.* They all three look.

And then in comes Paul Mulrooney, and his fiancee says, *Your parents have just been telling me how Clint Eastwood is Stan Laurel's son.*

You know, says Margaret, *the skinny one.*

Paul Mulrooney looks, and then he says, *Ah, yer mad, both of yez, and you too for listening. Let's go down to the pub.*

When they leave Jimmy sits next to Margaret and they watch Clint Eastwood point his gun at them. Jimmy says again, *Sure, look at the face on him.*

What It's Like to Sing in Irish

1. *Mo Ghile Mear* (My Lively Lad)
What the eye sees, the tongue
never says, but what the tongue says
the body knows:
the hot flint of hatred
lies under love's tender skin.

2. *Seacht nDólás na Maighdine Muire* (The Seven Sorrows of Mary)
The words leave the tongue
and enter the ear
sharper for being unseen,
as the Virgin's tears for her crucified son
fall onto flagstones
pooled with the blood
of the Easter Rising.

3. *Éiníní* (Little Birds)
The words seen while singing:
scissors in a mirror,
blades moving toward
instead of away
like the beaks of birds.

4. *Máire Ní Brunaill* (Mary Brunall)
The more I sing, the clearer they become,
those faces in a mirror
on a wattle wall.

The last defense of the Irish
is their durable tongue,
where *yes* is rare,
and the word for *no*
is the language itself.

At the Arraignment

The courtroom walls are bare and the prisoner wears
a plastic bracelet, like in a hospital. Jesus stands beside him.
The bailiff hands the prisoner a clipboard and he puts his
thumbprint on the sheet of white paper. The judge asks,

What is your monthly income? *A hundred dollars.*
How do you support yourself? *As a carpenter, odd jobs.*
Where are you living? *My friend's garage.*
What sort of vehicle do you drive? *I take the bus.*
How do you plead? *Not guilty.* The judge sets bail
and a date for the prisoner's trial, calls for the interpreter
so he may speak to the next prisoners.
In a good month I eat, the third one tells him.
In a bad month I break the law.

The judge sighs. The prisoners
are led back to jail with a clink of chains.
Jesus goes with them. More prisoners
are brought before the judge.

Jesus returns and leans against the wall near us,
gazing around the courtroom. The interpreter reads a book.
The bailiff, weighed down by his gun, stands
with arms folded, alert and watchful.
We are only spectators, careful to speak
in low voices. We are so many. If we make a sound,
the bailiff turns toward us, looking stern.

The judge sets bail and dates for other trials,
bringing his gavel down like a little axe.

Jesus turns to us. *If you won't help them,* he says,
then do this for me. Dress in silks and jewels,
and then go naked. Be stoic, and then be prodigal.
Lead exemplary lives, then go down into prison
and be bound in chains. Which of us has never broken a law?
I died for you — a desperate extravagance, even for me.
If you can't be merciful, at least be bold.

The judge gets up to leave.

The stern bailiff cries, *All rise.*

World Politics

Trudy's cat Norma Jean is always behind me when I back down the driveway and she never knows what to do. She runs straight down the concrete in the path of the car, only at the last minute thinking to hop into the flowers or jump the fence. Sometimes she runs all the way down and only turns when she gets to the sidewalk. She seems to see no other course.

If Norma Jean didn't reach the sidewalk, she'd be squashed under the wheels of the car and it would be my fault, and I would be furious, mad enough to kill her. Trudy would come out of her house and scream at me and cry. I'd cry. I'd be sad to see Norma Jean crushed on the driveway, her little body flattened, her blood-soaked fur, her pink intestines spread out on the concrete for all to see, everyone in the neighborhood standing around watching the pitiful scene. *It was her own fault!* I would shout, feeling guilty.

The car is huge and loud. Even when I go slowly, the car is an elephant trumpeting through the jungle of the yard. Can't she see it coming? Can't she hear it? Can't she realize what to do? She panics, the tires roll closer, the engine roars, the backup lights blaze. I rev the motor to warn her, I honk the horn. *For God's sake, Norma Jean, here comes disaster!* But she's like the girl in the horror movie, so enthralled by doom she can only stand and scream, until even flowers are no longer an option.

Ode to Thelma Ritter

When you watch *Rear Window* or *All About Eve,*
it's not Thelma you see. You see Grace Kelly.
You see Anne Baxter. You see Bette Davis, dazzling
even in middle age. Thelma
never dazzles. Young or old, she doesn't wear
shimmering gowns or spike-heeled shoes.
Onscreen, while the others pose and talk,
Thelma gets to work, pouring drinks, making coffee.
After Bette Davis, in romantic twilight,
gives her Oscar-winning speech, Thelma
flicks on the lights. Let's remember
real life, she says. Let's not forget its harsh
lessons. My face, for instance, and the fact
that no matter how good I am in this movie,
you won't remember me.

In *Rear Window* Thelma wears
a plain dress and flat brown shoes, and she is
beautiful the way one small dahlia is beautiful,
lovely as a spear of wheat or a single perfect
Brussels sprout. She's like the cat
that stares at you and suddenly
you remember times you let people down.
When Thelma speaks, you want to do better,
to make something of your life. She's no goddess,
but she's no stooge. She's the cow in the pasture
where three fickle mares step gracefully toward you,
hoping for sugar. She's the level meadow leading up
to the rugged but feckless snow-capped peaks. She is
the clear cold stream the sleek trout of your dreams swims in.

I Plan to Grow Old at the St. George Hotel

for Gray Chang

In skin as heavy as silk I'll lie
along the sill a story above the street.
A player will carry his keyboard under one arm
in search of a band, the bubble man
will set up tub, ready sticks with their loop of string,
a siren call like a long-dead friend, a thief
sip his sweet take from a fragrant cup. I'll watch
a magician bring a dead dove back to life
while the harper tunes beneath the hummed surprise.
A unicyclist will sing the newest song, lamps come on,
lovers stroll whispering, skin against skin
through the spangled night. Bubbles will rise
and glow, paned spheres against the light.
The magician will stroke the feathers of the dove,
love fly arrow-straight from the harper's strings,
my skin settle into dust above.

Looking for You

The stones move by like tiny houses.
I could stroll through here like a giant.

Am I on the right road? Where are you now?
I drive slowly, looking for a stone near a tree.

Your voice, by some mistake, rehearsed an old message.
Hand to mouth I listened, scalp prickling.

I don't remember where you are among all these trees.
When I find you I'll lie flat on the ground above you.

The disease, misdirected, found you by mistake.
It's so hard to ask directions in this place.

Music Lesson

for Gene Lewis (1940-2000)

He asks, Can you imagine the notes before you sing them? I can
remember them afterwards, I say. Good, he says, because it's the
same thing. You just do it in reverse, look forward instead of
back. The music glides along, and you imagine what comes next.
But the music only flows one way, I say. What if I miss my
entrance? You won't miss it, he says. I have trouble diving in, I
say. You don't have to dive in, he says, you're already there. We're
all already there—the players, the conductor, the singers, we're
there in the water all the time. All you have to do is start swimming.

I'm stuck on the bank, yet I sing when he plays the first measures
on the piano. He sings with me, and he's right, I'm in the water.
He follows me as closely as a bird follows its shadow along the
smooth surface of a river. *Oh Lamb of God,* we sing. He sings the
chorus part too, tilting back his head, *Oh Lamb of God, have mercy.*
Have mercy upon us. He plays the orchestra part, a warm undercurrent.
I float along easily.

When we finish he leaves his fingers on the keys awhile, letting
the last notes ring. He inclines his head toward me, a nod of
praise, and smiles. Good, that was good, he says. You see? Just
remember in reverse. Try it once more. Hands back on the keyboard,
he begins again, turning back time. He bows toward the keys as
he plays, smiling faintly, humming a little, hearing in his head all
the instruments of the orchestra, all the voices.

Even now, this is how I imagine him.

On the Lake Shore Limited

Thundering out of Chicago three hours late into Indiana past
midnight, clothes rumpled, tempers frayed, lounge car sold out, smell of
sewage and rancid grease, behind the counter a guy juggling cellophaned
sandwiches like a vaudevillian, slapping pizza in the microwave, yellow formica
countertop under the grime and harsh light, a faint cool breeze, a late night
chill around the eyes, muscles trembling, everybody total strangers at a
carnival, exhausted, grinning, up late like jazz musicians jamming, something's
about to happen, this is it, this is where to be, three guys singing bebop by
the cinnamon rolls, feet tapping, shoulders swaying, a guy wailing the
formica countertop like bongos, Chuck Berry, Little Richard, rhythm
of the tracks, ding of the microwave, and we speed on into Ohio like a song

New Hampshire

Something about the sky, how blue it is,
how the clouds come and go, how not even the hills
interrupt it. Lars lies on his back staring up
and says it reminds him of Sweden. Same
latitude, I say, and he says maybe, but maybe
it's something else, and we both look up.

I walk under this sky in the woods and meet
not a soul and think maybe it has to do with
humans per square foot. This is the sky
from my childhood, the sky over
the Santa Susana Mountains before smog,
the sky above Santa Cruz before the land craze,
before the housing boom. When people moved west,
the sky moved back to New Hampshire and resumed
its life of lightning and stars. Lars lies on the hill at night,
looks at the Milky Way distinct and festive
and wonders what to do with his life
under such a sky.

Shaker Hall at Watervliet

for Shelley Phillips

When I sing this wooden hall becomes
my head, my voice the air
in every corner. A fever
spreads from my feet
to my chest, and space
curves along the song so I touch
the ceiling and all the walls at once,
like setting fingers on stars.
I find the notes by feel, the tune
solid as the floor. I sing
and the song appears
like dust in sunlight,
like a dream but stronger
and more handsome, a song
always there but only seen
when sung, my feet
still warm when I'm done.

Four Nocturnes by Georges de La Tour
1630-1640

1. *The Magdalen with Two Flames*
She has taken off her jewels by candlelight,
set the knotted strand of pearls
on the table by the mirror—

the pearl earring,
the two bracelets like glittering snakes
have slipped to the floor

as the spices slipped from her fingers
at his tomb. She stares

not at the skull she cradles in her lap,
but toward the mirror, at the short candle's flame
and its mirrored flame.

2. *The Magdalen at the Mirror*
She has bared one shoulder,
has let her dark hair down.

She touches the skull as one blind,
resting her fingers in its sockets, her eyes
on the skull's bright image. She sees

how the face without flesh is still a face,
how bone lives another life in the right light,

how the skull is always there
under the skin.

3. *The Magdalen with the Smoking Flame*
Shoulders bare above the loosened blouse,
her skin amber in the light,
she holds the skull on her lap

and looks past the lamp and the rough wooden cross,
past the books, the whip of knotted rope,

recalls how they rolled the stone against the tomb,
how she leaned on it and wept,

how the stone rolled away.

He is the hardest jewel, making
a light at the back of her eyes.
She is sharp-edged as sorrow,
staring into the dark.

4. *The Repentant Magdalen*
She caresses the skull
like a lover's face,
gazing into its eyes
with her hidden eyes.

She says to the skull, *Oh my dear,*
oh my dear. It is as beautiful to her now
as when it wore its flesh and nothing else.
So beautiful, the flesh, the hollow bone,

that with her hair loose like smoke
and her body bare, she gazes.

The Library at Alexandria

In the city of the world the gates of sun and moon
are always open, and bright against a rainless sky
shines the white dome of the Serapeum
where we keep the world in books. Babylonians

speak of *zero* and give the world its nothing,
but we give the world itself, and give it
forever. Each day inside the Serapeum, Enkidu
quarrels with Gilgamesh, Odysseus sails for home,
Abraham abandons Ishmael to hold the knife
forever above Isaac's heart. Here Atlas
shoulders the world our city gives him, here

Krishna holds the lotus where the world sleeps.
We know what lies at the heart of life
and have built our city around it,
no city so unique, no people
so favored by fortune.

When conquerors with vast armies come,
we bow to them but roll our eyes, Caesar in shining armor
stripped by our wit. Young men more beautiful than our city
die defending it, but our books never fade.
The works of Manetho, of Mochus the Phoenician,

Ephesus of Pergamum, Menander of Tyre—who
can imagine the world without them?
Rigid skins of scrolls too tough to burn
live long past generals. Our marble walls, the Nile,
our tiled roofs and stone canals surround these books.
If young men die, more will come, more books

to tell the stories of their lives. What is *zero*? Where
is *nothing*? Look around! Daily among the goats and melons,
among the hyacinths in our markets, poets sing
songs in every tongue, and all night long
astronomers wander through our perfumed stars.

Egyptian and Roman, Greek and Jew, all are welcome here,
even the dead, young dead in the fields, thousands
cut down with sword and spear while more are born
safe in our city of the world, thick-walled and winding,
tough and moist, impossible to burn.

We know what lies at the heart of life.

Open Spaces

The tarred road turns to dirt, then disappears. Lichen
on granite. Scorpions, lizards, snakes. Tumbleweeds
roll over bare fields to the hills. Sage on stony mountains,
whiteoaks brush the sky. No human thing, no green except
what grows where sparse water goes. The summer air
full of crows and insects droning, oven-hot
with a smell of dust and dry rock. The winter air
frosty, a sharp cold, clean as the future. Nothing
but earth and sky.

You could stand in a field then and see at your feet
little fist-size clods with their own little shadows.
Young corn grew knee high all the way to the hills,
grew high above your head. When you drove past cornfields
with the car window down you could feel
the change in the air, the moist leaves breathing.
When cornstalks stiffened and grew brittle,
rustling and knocking together like old bones, the air
went dry again, then the razed fields brown and waiting,
flat as forever.

We were out beyond the cowboys and the gold mines, way out
in a West full of orange trees, avocados, the cinema. We were in
the terrain of the alien planet, the hills of Galilee, the England
of Robin Hood, the South Korea of Hawkeye Pierce. Those rolling
meadows you see, those barren mountains, that's where I lived,
those open spaces.

I used to stand in a field of wild asparagus, feet among thick stems,
their lacy ferns waving as far as I could see. They're all
gone now. Fields of tumbleweed, sagebrush, corn—torn up,
all houses now, hotels, high-rises, malls, all vertical, even the horizon.
Sometimes in old films I see them again, those fields
through the buildings at the edge of a city. Sometimes
I hear a rumor about a frontier, and I set my pen on an empty page
like taking a step in the old valley, nothing but bare sweet
ground stretching out until it meets the hills.
Just earth. Sky.

Paradise

I heard a song about cinnamon,
got hungry to suck its peeled bark,
to feel the bite of distant spice on my tongue,
and my hunger drove me down to the sea
where I took ship as a common sailor
and for weeks sucked hardtack, swabbed decks,
stared at the horizon. At night, sniffing the wind,

I sang with the crew, then heard in my dreams
strange tunes played through a reeded brass,
a metal mermaid calling me out of my skin,
the voice of the horizon—but only woke
to the scrape of keel on sand,
a rumble of wooden wheels,
the smell of salt cod stewed
on a seaweed fire. In the new land

all the work was done down mines,
so I took up a pick and swung it
and swung it and swung it, and one day
held in my hand a nugget, a yearning
for a country not overrun
with sailors turned miners,
for a land more treed than peopled.
I heard a new song that went

If what you want you can't find,
and what you find you can't love,
then let what you love

drive you down to the sea.

Acknowledgements

Without any one of these people, this book would not have been made. I thank them all, with all my heart, and will spend the rest of my life (except in the case of the network executives) endeavoring to deserve them:

Hummingbirds Julia Alter, Jonell Jel'enedra, George Lober, Joanna Martin, Tilly Shaw, and especially Ken Weisner and Len Anderson
Hummingbird Joseph McNeilly, who convinced me to do this
Joseph Stroud and all the students in his Cabrillo College workshops from 1997 to 2003
Writers Barbara Bloom, Paula Jones, Ana Chou, John Chandler, Wilma Chandler, Ed Sams, Mort Marcus, Dona Luongo Stein, Anita Wilkins, Alliee DeArmond, Mary Lonnberg Smith, Joan Zimmerman, and Allen Berg
Writers David Sullivan, Rosie King, and Charles Atkinson
Dennis Morton, Len Anderson and everyone at Poetry Santa Cruz
Paul Fahey and *Mindprints*, in whose pages two of these poems first appeared
Patrice Vecchione, Amber Coverdale Sumrall and *In Celebration of the Muse*
Kirby Wilkins, Stan Rushworth, David Sullivan and the *Porter Gulch Review*, in whose pages many of these poems first appeared
Ken Weisner, Jeff Tagami and *Quarry West*, in whose pages two of these poems appeared
E. A. Parsons' *The Alexandrian Library* for wording in "The Library at Alexandria"
Writers Robert Wells and Chris Pundeff
Writing teachers Caroline Nakamura, Marion Rheimbold, Nils Peterson, and Joseph Stroud
Musicians Shelley Phillips, Barry Phillips, Lars Johannesson, Janet Herman, Galt Barber, William Coulter, Merry Dennehy, Clay Cambern, Jonathan Crump, Jane Hancock and everyone at Community Music School of Santa Cruz
Music teachers Paul Hillier, Harlan Hokin, Kent Nagano, and Gene Lewis
St. John the Baptist Episcopal Church, especially William Visscher, Fr. Steve Ellis, Fr. Bill Rainford, Anne Wallace Baker, Bill Kell, Carrie Hanson, and the Rev. Eliza Linley
Artist Juliette Aristides, for her kind permission to use her painting on the cover
The network executives who canceled *The Tick, Firefly, Watching Ellie, EZ Street, Sports Night, The Job, Bakersfield P.D., Action*, and *Lucky*, giving me time to write
Deborah Shulman, Richard Griffiths, Jefferson Hancock, Joanna Santana-Bates and everyone at the Learning Skills Program of Cabrillo College
The baristas at The Buttery, Lulu Carpenter's, Kelly's Bakery, and Java Junction
The makers of Ficklin's Port
Candace Fields, Christian Q. Ness, Cherrie de Voogdt, and Ed Johnsrud
Joan Safajek, who saved my life
My parents Rose and B. C. Spencer, my siblings Randall Spencer and Kimberly Mulrooney
Lin Rolens, who rescued this book at a crucial phase
Clare Rolens and Sam Rolens, for whom the window they flew out of is always open
and Jim Rolens: "Nought beneath the skie more sweet, more worthy"
—Book VI, *The Odyssey* (tr. Chapman)

Debra Spencer invented her own alphabet when she was three. She wrote her first book in the second grade and went on to earn a BA from the University of California at Santa Cruz in 1972 and an MA from San Jose State University in 1988, where she won the Anne Lillis Memorial Scholarship for Poetry. In her desk she keeps a Bart Giammati baseball card, a fossilized shark's tooth, the tuning key to an Anglian harp, and a piece of the Berlin Wall. She works at Cabrillo College as a learning disabilities specialist, and sings with Community Music School of Santa Cruz.